SEXUAL ABUSE
And Its Implications For Church And Society

Breaking the Silence

REV. DR. ANGELLA A. WORGES

ISBN: 9798351345383 (paperback)

Printed in the United States of America.

This book is dedicated to those women who confided in me and even those who continue to bear their pain in silence.

Acknowledgment

With a heart of gratitude, I express thanks to some persons who have contributed to the successful completion of this work.

Thanks to my husband, Oswald, for his constant support and encouragement.

Thanks to the library staff at the Jamaica Theological Seminary and the United Theological College.

Thanks to Doctor Kathleen O'Connor and the Library staff at the Colombia Theological Seminary in Atlanta, Georgia.

Special thanks to my brethren at the Glengoffe Church of God of Prophecy who believed in me.

About the Author

Reverend Doctor Angella Worges is a graduate of Columbia Theological Seminary in Atlanta, Georgia, USA, where she completed doctoral studies in Ministry and Religious Studies. She holds a Master of Arts Degree in Counselling Psychology from the Caribbean Graduate School of Theology and a Bachelor's Degree from the Jamaica Theological Seminary in General Studies with an emphasis on Counselling. She also holds a teaching diploma from Shortwood Teacher's College, where she focused on Secondary School Education, majoring in Linguistics and Literature.

Reverend Doctor Worges has been a teacher for thirty-seven years, a lecturer for ten years, an adjunct counselor at the Family Life Ministries for seventeen years (an institution that is committed to the advancement of family life), and the head of the Behavioural and Sciences Department at the Jamaica Theological Seminary. She is also a pastor in the Church of God of Prophecy.

Reverend Doctor Worges has been personally involved in working with women as she serves in different ministries in the church as well as in her professional capacity as a counselor. She is a Marriage Officer, Justice of the Peace, and a counselor.

She is now a widow after being married to Oswald for thirty-eight years. She is the mother of five sons and a daughter.

Table of Contents

Introduction

After hearing a message at church about the trauma faced by Tamar, David's daughter (see 2 Samuel 13), a twenty-eight-year-old woman paid me a visit. Like a robot, she walked into the room and stared off into space. Then she took a seat and, without any prompting, she began to speak.

> ***"Pastor, do you know who took my virginity? It was my father. I was just eleven years old. I had just passed my exams to enter high school. He told me that before I went out into the wider world, he had to teach me what real love was. He cautioned me to keep it between us because people who love each other keep this kind of secret between them. He proceeded to undress me…"***

The father in question was a pastor. She was breaking her silence for the first time and could recall her experiences vividly. The pain of the abortions she endured was so very real.

Sexual abuse is a common phenomenon in Jamaican society. This type of abuse is defined by the *American Heritage Dictionary* as "the forcing of unwanted sexual activity by one person on another by using threats or coercion or sexual activity that is deemed improper or harmful, as between an adult and a minor or with a person of diminished mental capacity." Kee MacFarlane, in discussing child sexual abuse, felt that both legal and medical definitions of sexual abuse are thought to be restrictive since they frequently rely on physical evidence of molestation, which is usually not present, particularly with preschoolers, where penetration occurs less frequently than with older children.[1]

The true magnitude of this problem is not highlighted because many individuals have remained silent for varying reasons, among which is a culture of silence that surrounds sexual malpractice in Jamaican society. Several factors have contributed to this silence. One such reason is the stigma that is attached to sexually abused victims. They are often viewed as damaged property and sometimes become the subject of ridicule. Therefore, because of guilt and shame they keep silent.

Also, evident in the society is the fact that many acts of sexual abuse are committed by family members. The victims are encouraged to keep silent to protect the family name. In other words, they are saving the family

---

[1] Kee MacFarlane, Sexual *Abuse of Young Children (*London: Holt, Rinehart and Winston, 1986), 4.

from embarrassment. When acts of sexual abuse are committed in the church, they are also suppressed to protect the integrity of the church.

There are also times when survivors of sexual abuse are threatened. This results in them bearing the pain of their trauma in silence to protect their lives and/or the lives of their loved ones. This culture of silence has caused many women to carry emotional scars for several years, sometimes taking them through the years of childhood into their adult years. This also allows for perpetrators of sexual abuse to go unidentified and unpunished, thereby facilitating the continuation of this undesirable behavior.

The colonial past of the region has also socialized men to be abusers of women. Jamaica, like other Caribbean countries, is referred to as a plantation society. These societies have certain common features, such as male dominance over female sexuality. This behavior was encouraged by colonial masters to allow women to become pregnant, thereby increasing the labor force for the plantation. Slave women were even given incentives to perform this task.[2] This socialized behavior is still evident in today's society. Raymond T.

---

[2] George L. Beckford, *Persistent Poverty: Underdevelopment in Plantation Economics* (New York: Oxford University Press, 1972), 59.

Smith, in speaking about these societies, alludes to the fact that people in these societies are already socially formed with a culture and a set of attitudes that need to be reformed.[3]

Survivors of this crime vary across age groups, social class, ethnic background, and religious affiliation. The perpetrators themselves are from different backgrounds, including caregivers, family members, law enforcement officers, church leaders, and other individuals, known and unknown. Many of these victims, as well as the perpetrators, are church people. The church, therefore, must interact with them daily.

Within the Jamaican culture, there are myths that perpetuate sexual abuse. One such myth is a feeling among some individuals that if a man has been infected with a sexually transmitted disease and has sexual intercourse with a virgin, he will be cured of this disease. The belief in such a myth has caused many young girls to have sexual intercourse forced upon them. There is also the feeling among some fathers and stepfathers that they should be the first to get sexual satisfaction from their daughters, who they have worked so hard to maintain.

---

[3] Raymond T. Smith, "Social Stratification, Cultural Pluralism and Integration in West Indian Societies," in *Caribbean Integration*, eds. S. Lewis and T.G. Matthews (Rio Piedras:Puerto Rico,1967),230.

In addition to the above-mentioned myths and beliefs existing in Jamaica, there is a growing trend in the media network that encourages sexual abuse. This author refers to this as a "sex-saturated society." The media has played its role in perpetuating this situation as there is a media culture with much sexual innuendo. The female anatomy is often used by various media houses as an advertising tool. This is evident in the fact that the female's body is used for advertising a variety of goods and services that sometimes do not even seem associated with what is being advertised. The female is often portrayed to be on sale.

Music also contributes to the perpetuation of sexual abuse. Music is an integral part of the Jamaican culture and through this medium, cultural values and norms are passed on. In many instances, women are portrayed in a very negative light through music, particularly where their sexuality is concerned. In recent times, effort has been made to place a ban on certain types of music being played via the media houses. However, the public transportation system as well as the dancehall culture that exists in the society has allowed many individuals to view women in a negative light based on derogatory statements made about them through music. This medium does not promote a positive image of female sexuality.

Working with victims of sexual abuse while completing the practicum component of my doctoral degree in Ministry has revealed that the church, for varying reasons, is not placing enough emphasis on this situation. It was also discovered that child sexual abuse has far-reaching effects and that even adults who were survivors of child sexual abuse carry the scars into adulthood.

This book examines sexual abuse and its effects on victims. It will also serve as a means of sensitizing the church population, particularly church leaders, on the extent of sexual abuse and its effects on individuals. By understanding the trauma suffered by victims of sexual abuse, the church should be able to plan programs to help these victims by:

(a) Diagnosing these cases.
(b) Developing strategies for ministering to these individuals.
(c) Making appropriate referrals so the victims can receive adequate professional help.

Theoretical Commitments, Perspective, and Methodology

In completing the introductory seminar for the Doctor of Ministry Degree, my target group identified the need for a strong counseling ministry. Before I was appointed as pastor, theological training was not considered important in my denomination. The general feeling was that the Holy Spirit would fix all things as long as we fasted, prayed, and read only the Bible. However, with my exposure to theological training and the introduction of counseling in the church program, I now feel that counseling would contribute to a more holistic ministry that would meet the mental health needs of individuals within the ministry setting. The courses "Church and Society" and "Church as a Cooperate Witness" further helped me to see the need for a counseling ministry. I therefore decided to do my practicum in counseling.

My practicum experience provided more insight into the need for a counseling ministry. During the practicum, I became aware of an overwhelming number of cases of sexual abuse. Many of these individuals were referred to me for counseling by church leaders who themselves do not have the expertise to minister to these individuals.

Following the completion of my practical experience, I studied the book of Genesis. I found myself drawn to the many acts of sexual abuse against women in biblical culture. Reflecting on the theology postulated by Karl Barth and David Bosh, I endorse the theological school of thought that claims the church must be relevant to the community where it exists. Karl

Barth, for instance, spoke about the changing stages and situations throughout human history that the community of Jesus Christ should address.[4] Bosh, on the other hand, spoke about the missionary paradigm that has to do with reinterpreting mission in present circumstances.[5] I recognize that this is one role that the church should be playing. I also believe that ministry is service as was exemplified by Jesus (see Luke 22:27).

In my various professional capacities that includes Associate Counselor at the Family Life Ministries (a nondenominational counseling institution in Jamaica), Christian Education Director for the Church of God of Prophecy in Jamaica and the Cayman Islands, and Parish Counseling and Family Ministries Director for churches in the parish of St. Catherine, I am cognizant of the fact that on the odd occasions when pastors and church workers are made aware of instances of sexual abuse, they tend to refer individuals for counseling because they are not equipped with the necessary expertise to minister to these individuals. It is therefore my intention to help pastors and other church workers

---

[4] Karl Barth, *Church Dogmatics: The Doctrine of Reconciliation,*1V.3.2. Eds. G.W. Bromiley and T.F. Torrance (London. New York: T&T Clark International, 2004),831.

[5] David J. Bosch, *Transforming Missions: Paradigm Shifts in Theology of Mission* (Mary Knoll, New York: Orbis Books, 2005), 113.

minister to these individuals by answering these questions:

- What are the effects of sexual abuse on these survivors?
- Is the church meeting the needs of survivors of sexual abuse?
- What strategies can the church employ in helping these survivors?

By using qualitative research methodology, I conducted interviews with professionals in the field who have been working with victims of sexual abuse. I also conducted a survey in my church and among a group of theological students at the Jamaica Theological Seminary, where at the time I was an adjunct lecturer. Questionnaires were used to conduct the survey. Professionals working in the field of counseling were chosen for interviews because of their practical experience in working with persons in the Jamaican society.

The survey was conducted in two different ministry settings to get a true picture of a wider cross-section of the situation as it really exists. The seminary setting was selected for the survey because it also represents different denominational groups, thus providing a better understanding of sexual abuse as it exists in other denominations.

Sexual Abuse Heritage From Scriptures

Scriptural evidence[6] suggests that the matter of sexual abuse has existed from as far back as in God's chosen family and has been identified in many instances throughout salvation history. One of the first identified incidences of biblical sexual abuse is the case of Sarah, Abraham's wife. Although Abraham was chosen by God to be the head of His chosen family, it can be said that Abraham exposed his wife to sexual abuse. In an effort to protect himself, Abraham willingly gave over his wife to the exploits of Pharaoh, king of Egypt (see Genesis 12:11-16).

Abraham seemed to benefit from this move as not only was his life spared, but he received financial gain. According to Spangler and Syswerda, he was paid for his wife's services with the currency of the day.[7] Like so many other individuals in today's Jamaican society, Abraham readily accepted the benefits gained from his exploitation of women in that he accepted the gifts and readily went on his way with them. God, however, was not silent on this issue, since, according to the

---

[6] All scriptural references are taken from New Revised Standard Version, the New Annotated Bible with Apocrypha, Eds. Bruce M. Metzger and Roland E. Murphy (New York: Oxford University Press),1994.

[7] Spangler and Syswerda, 26.

scriptures, God moved to afflict Pharaoh because of Sarah (see Genesis 12:17).

Sexual exploitation/abuse against women seemed to be the accepted norm in Abraham's household. The case of Hagar, the slave girl of Sarah, can be cited as another instance of sexual abuse/exploitation (see Genesis 16). Sarah made the decision to give over the young virgin named Hagar to the exploits of her husband in order to make up for her own inadequacies. Abraham readily agreed to his wife's plan.

One can easily argue that this was the tradition of the day, as instances of similar practices have been found in the chosen family. Another example is in the case of Jacob, Abraham's grandson. Jacob's wives made their servants perform a function similar to the service Hagar offered Abraham (see Genesis 30:3-12). In each of these cases, as is the case in Jamaica, it was the weaker or dependent individuals who were being sexually exploited by those who held power over them.

Unlike other individuals of her time, however, Hagar was not accepting of her plight but rebelled as a result of what had been done to her (see Genesis 16:4). On this point I disagree with Spangler and Syswerda, who felt that Hagar's contempt for her mistress was because of pride in bearing the child that Sarah so badly wanted to bear.[8] What could prompt a girl of her position to be lauding things over her mistress when she very well knew that she depended on her mistress for survival? Her behavior could definitely be considered as rebellion because of rape. This theory seems to be supported by Delores Williams. She cited the fact that the word used to describe Hagar in Genesis 16 is ***sipha,*** which is translated to mean "*a virgin, dependent maid who serves the mistress of the house.*" Williams wrote:

> **This means that Hagar was a virgin when she was made to lie down with Abraham. Female slaves, especially those owned by slave masters, were often rented out as concubines by their masters. Obviously, Sarah had not allowed such a fate to befall Hagar. Could it be that Hagar, because of her Egyptian heritage and her protection against rape by Sarai, had status among other female slaves? Did she lose pride and status because of Sarai's betrayal of her virginity? Could it be that Hagar's argument with Sarai had nothing to do with her wanting to take over Sarai's position with Abraham, but that Sarai's betrayal of her would become obvious when her pregnancy by Abraham became obvious? Could it be that both women were concerned about a loss of status but for a different reason? Could it be that in the consciousness of foreign slaves like**

[8] Spangler and Syswerda, 32

> **Hagar, there was no particular value assigned to female slaves on the basis of their reproducing babies who became the property of the slave owners?**[9]

If these questions were to be answered in the affirmative, then this very situation describes an aspect of the Jamaican heritage that is linked to the colonial past of the nation. Under the colonial system, not only did slave masters rape their female slaves, but they also encouraged other slaves to do the same in order to produce. These babies would become the property of the plantation owners, thereby increasing the master's labour force.

It is against such a system that Hagar rebelled. She faced the circumstances of her rebellion when she was banished from her home. Again, God was seen moving in support of this victim of sexual abuse. It was depicted that God appeared in person to bring comfort to Hagar (see Genesis16:7-12; 21:17-19). In this I can agree with Spangler and Syswerda, who stated:

> **Hagar still had one thing going for her that her mistress never enjoyed: a personal relationship with God, who lovingly**

---

[9] Deloris Williams, *Sisters in the Wilderness* (New York: Orbis Books, 1993), 17.

> **intervened on her behalf, not once but twice. It happened when she was alone and afraid, without a shekel to her name.**[10]

Another instance of sexual abuse occurred in Jacob's family when Dinah, Jacob's daughter, went to visit other women in the community. It was reported that she was raped by Shechem, son of the ruler of the area (see Genesis 34). Evidently, this was not considered to be appropriate behavior when it happened outside of Israel because Dinah's brothers plotted and killed the offenders to avenge the act committed against their sister.

Tamar, another daughter of Israel, David's daughter, was also raped. In this instance, the offender was Tamar's half-brother, Ammon (see 2 Samuel 13). Tamar's pleas to her brother were to no avail. She was very cognizant of the fact that this action of her brother towards her would mean a life of desolation given the culture of her time. Her value as a woman was lost. Her father could no longer claim a bride price for her. Her very dignity as a woman and her usual place in her father's household was lost because she was now confined to a lesser position in her brother's house.

---

[10] Spangler and Syswerda, 32

Spangler and Syswerda, in assessing this situation, stated that Tamar's rape by Ammon did not begin to communicate the humiliation and despair that rape brought to those who experienced it. Tamar's pleas to her brother to refrain from the violation echo the sentiments of women through hundreds of years who have been forced into sexual acts against their will. Ammon, like many other men, was able to assault Tamar because he was stronger.[11] Absalom's response was typically that of many family members of sexually abused women. Although he was furious to the point where he later killed his half-brother for his actions, Absalom entreated Tamar to keep quiet, thereby forcing her to deal with her emotional turmoil all by herself.

One also needs to take into consideration David's non-response to the rape of his daughter by his very own son, her brother. In discussing sexual abuse in the church today, Neil and Thea Ormerod expressed some emotional feelings which might well have been experienced by these biblical women. They stated:

> **Becoming a victim of sexual abuse is a shattering experience. It undermines one's self-esteem, one's self of one's own dignity. It creates a burden of guilt and shame; guilt at**

[11] Spangler andSyswerda, 187.

> **the internalized sense that somehow one is to blame; shame at the thought of what one has endured and what people would say if they knew. Often it shatters one's personal boundaries, leaving one vulnerable to other abusive relationships... It disorients the victim leaving them unable to trust their own experiences, and their own feelings. Their own basic trust in others has been violated.**[12]

The question could also be asked as to whether or not David, Ammon's father, was also a sexual offender, guilty of the sexual abuse of Bathsheba. As king, David used his power to summon Bathsheba into his chambers, where he became sexually involved with her (see 2 Samuel 11). God intervened in the person of the prophet Nathan. Nathan's metaphorical expression of Bathsheba suggested that she was innocent and David was an exploiter (see Genesis 12). This being the case, the incident with Tamar, his daughter, was fulfilled prophecy made by Nathan for David's punishment (see 2 Samuel 12:10). Could it be that David did not have the moral authority to address this issue? He himself had been convicted of a similar crime (see 2 Samuels 12:7-14). The Bible addresses generational sins in Exodus 20:5 by stating that "**...the iniquities of the**

[12] Neil Ormerod and Thea Ormerod, *When Ministers Sin: Sexual Abuse in the Church* (Alexander: Millennium Books, 1995)51.

fathers are visited upon the sons and daughters..." God does forgive sins, but the price must be paid. The pain of this situation must have been torture for David.

Scripture also records a brutal incident of rape in the time of the Judges (see Judges 19). A particular Levite was traveling with his concubine and was taken into the household of a member of the tribe of Benjamin to rest for the night. The men of the community, having learned of his presence, sought to have intercourse with him. In an effort to protect himself, the Levite gave over his concubine to them. They raped her for the night, and by morning she was dead. Here we see a man willing to allow the sexual abuse of a woman in an effort to protect himself. We also see this vicious act of gang rape by men who were counted as members of God's chosen nation. However, this act sparked outrage among other members of God's chosen family. Other tribes of Israel declared war against the tribe of Benjamin because the perpetrators of the gang rape were identified as members of the tribe of Benjamin.

It is evident that throughout salvation history, sexual abuse was not an accepted norm. Whenever incidents of this nature were identified, individuals usually rose to the defense of the victims. There were times when God intervened, as was the case with Sarah and Hagar. God also protested through individuals, as in the case of Bathsheba, where a protest was made through

Nathan. God's reaction to sexual abuse is evident throughout the scripture. It is noted that God allows for the protection of the victims and punishment of the perpetrators. This is specifically spoken to in the law (see Deuteronomy 22:25-30; Leviticus 18).

In spite of the many acts of sexual abuse against women in scripture and God moving to protect them, the issue seems to be an inherited culture. Israelite wisdom literature depicts this practice being continued where women were allowed to be abused. There is no doubt that during that period, women were considered to be in a subservient role in society.

K. E. Bailey, in discussing the status of women in that era, cited the work of Gail Shulman, which stated that the Talmud (the body of opinions and teachings of laws contained in the Torah) states that Talmudic laws grant women the status of a well-loved object or a slightly retarded child. In highlighting the plight of women, Shulman also quoted some Jewish prayers. The Jewish men would pray, "Blessed art though Lord our God, King of the Universe who has not made me a woman." The corresponding prayer for the female is "Blessed art thou O Lord our God, King of the universe who has made me according to thy will."[13]

---

[13] K.E. Bailey, *Women in Ben Sera and the New Testament*(Cleveland: Dillon/Lieder Bach, 1972)60.

In spite of the many examples of sexual abuse against women in the Bible, and the many examples cited which indicate that this was unacceptable behavior, this trauma continues to plague women in the church and the wider society. Women in the Jamaican society today experience the same trauma as was experienced by women like Dinah and Tamar in Israel. The incidence of sexual abuse, however, is often kept silent in the Jamaican society and in the church in particular.

This thought on the culture of silence was supported by Michelle-Ann Letman in the *Jamaica Daily Gleaner.* After conducting a survey among individuals who work with women and children, Letman stated that many cases of sexual abuse go unpunished because there is a culture of silence. This is caused by fear that in turn hinders persecution. She further stated that within the first nine months of the year 2008, the Child Development Agency received five hundred and forty-one (541) reports of carnal abuse. However, the police sex crime agency (Centre for the Investigation of Sexual Offenses and Child Abuse) recorded only two hundred and sixty-seven (267) cases of carnal abuse.[14] Most of these sex offenders go unpunished; therefore

[14] Letman, Michelle-Ann.2008.Carnal Abuse Hush UP: Fear Culture of Silence Hinders Persecution, Daily Gleaner, August 19.

victims, as in the case of Tamar, suffer this trauma in silence. Davis also gave support to the claim of a culture of silence that exists where sexual crimes are concerned. However, she has extended this culture of silence to the church when she stated that the church has too often been silent on the abuse of women and girls, even within church communities.[15]

This point brings into focus the fact that the church also has its share of sexual abuse. The Jamaican media has reported cases of sexual violence against women in the church and has even identified some perpetrators as church leaders. Even during the course of their search for this project, the media reported an upsurge of sexual abuse of women and children in society.

It is also a fact that many of these sex crimes are committed in the homes of individuals. Patricia Davis has cited a situation that is similar to the Jamaican context. She stated that these victims of sexual and physical abuse are mostly at risk from men they know, love, and trust. To emphasize her point, she quoted from the German journal *Emma*, which has documented that "The most dangerous place for western women is not the street but the privacy of the

---

[15]Patricia Davis, *Counseling Adolescent Girls* (Minneapolis:Augsburg Fortress, 1996), 66.

home." In discussing the matter of incest, Davis postulated:

> **The androcentric culture in which we live is the common but rarely articulated sense that the father in the family owns the other family members, especially the women and children. This belief which has even been upheld in our legal system, makes some men think that they are entitled to use and abuse family members for their own purpose and gratification. One of the most tragic of these abuses is incest, where a family member, usually male, takes advantage of his power over a weaker member, and coerces her into engaging in sexual acts with him. These acts can be oral, vaginal, or anal intercourse, or they can be fondling, inappropriate caressing, seductive or oral speech, forcing the child to watch or listen to pornographic materials, forcing the child to watch while the abuser masturbates or has sex with someone else, or making sexual comments about her body.**[16]

It is evident that incest and other forms of sexual abuse have spanned the different eras of human existence, although in the initial stages, the modern jargon was not

[16] Patricia Davis, 66.

used to describe these acts as sexual abuse. God, in working directly with people, addressed this issue. The onus is therefore on the church, which is God's representative, to deal with this issue today.

As was mentioned earlier, fifty questionnaires were administered to two separate groups in an effort to assess the true situation as it exists in Jamaican society today. One group, which comprised of thirty (30) individuals who represent ten percent (10%) of the adult and adolescent church population, was from my ministry setting. The sample was randomly selected using every tenth individual. The other group to which the questionnaire was administered was a class of twenty students at the Jamaica Theological Seminary. This class of students represents a wide cross-section of denominations in Jamaican society. The students were studying for their Bachelor of Arts degree. This group was comprised of teachers, social workers, and pastors. Individuals in the group were training for ministry, counseling or social work.

Interviews were conducted with some psychologists, as well as with a member of the Children Advocacy group. In order to determine the true magnitude of the problem, interviews were also conducted with members of the police department.

Research Findings

Questionnaire Results

A total of fifty persons completed the questionnaire. The age group and gender of the respondents are shown in figures 1 and 2 respectively.

Figure 3 shows the awareness of respondents to incidents of sexual abuse.

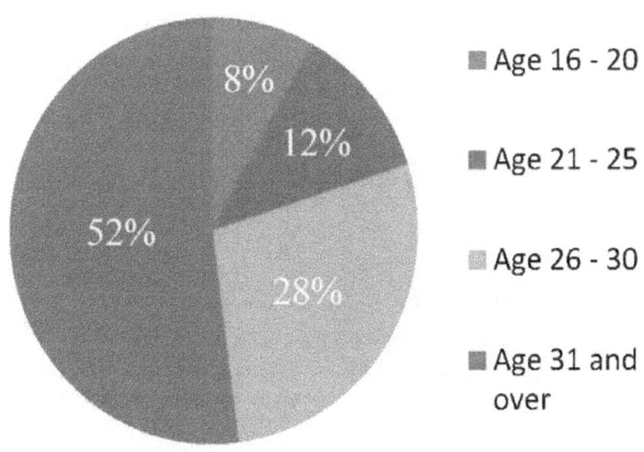

Figure 1. Age group of respondents.

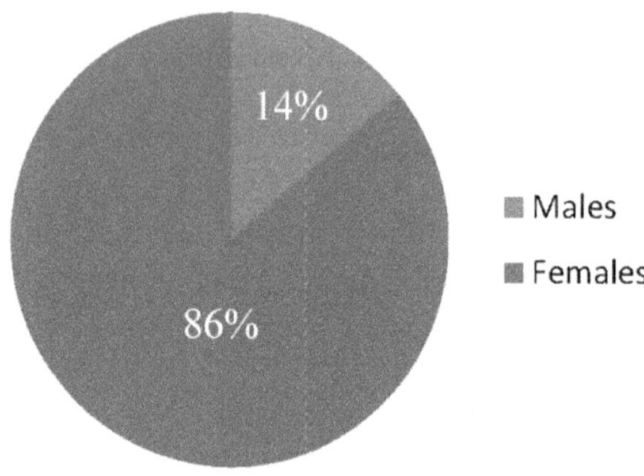

Figure 2. Gender of respondents

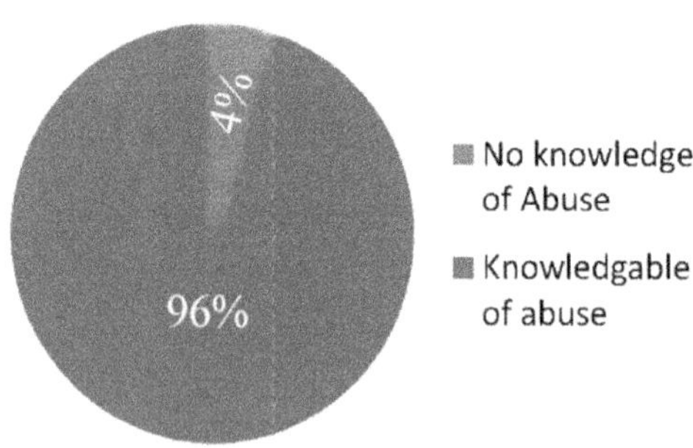

Figure 3. Awareness of respondents to sexual abuse

Of the males who responded to the questionnaire, three did not know anyone who was sexually abused, while only one female was not aware of anyone who had been sexually abused. This female respondent was in the age group 16-20 years.

Figure 4 shows the church status of each respondent. All the leaders were aware of cases of sexual abuse. Figure 5 shows the number of cases identified in each age group.

Member	Leader	Visitor
22	25	2

Figure 4. Church status of respondents

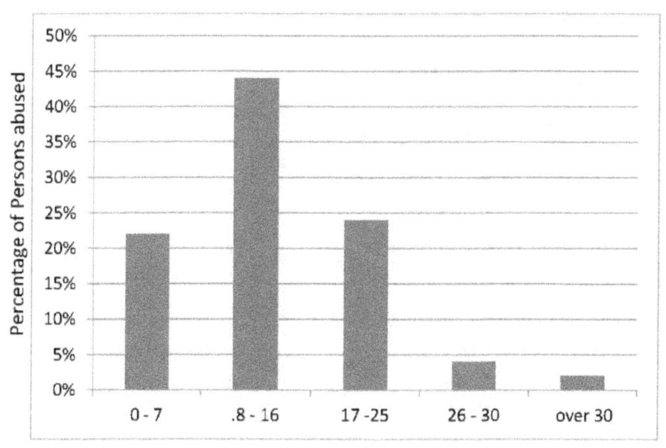

Figure 5. Percentage of Abuse by age group

Figure 6 shows the action taken by or on behalf of the abused.

Figure 7 shows the percentage of victims who knew their abusers.

Figure 8 shows the percentage of abusers who were related in some way to the victims.

Figure 9 shows the relationship between the abuser and the victim.

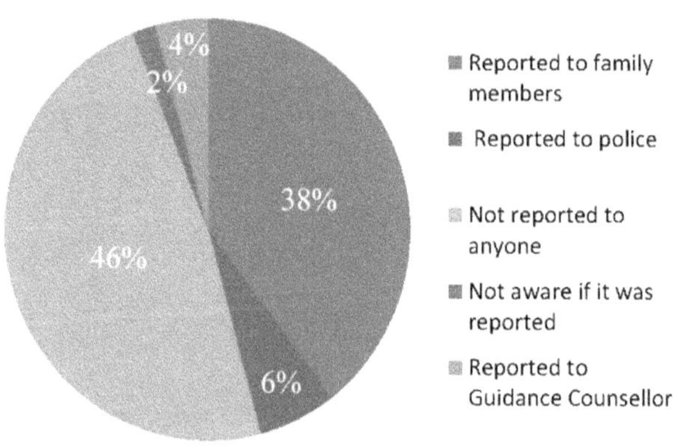

Figure 6. Action taken by or on behalf of abused women

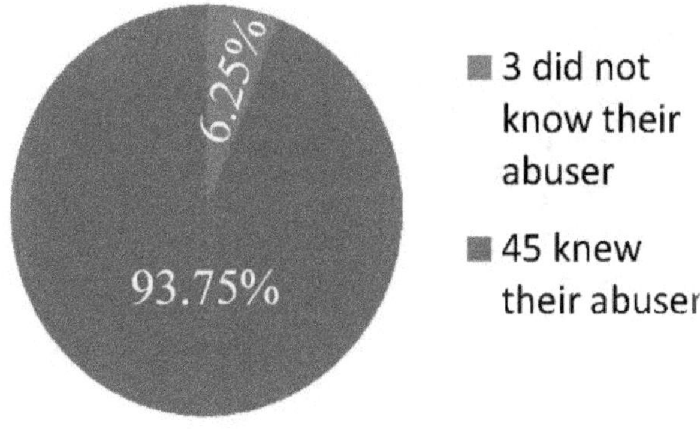

Figure 7
Percentage of victims who knew their abusers

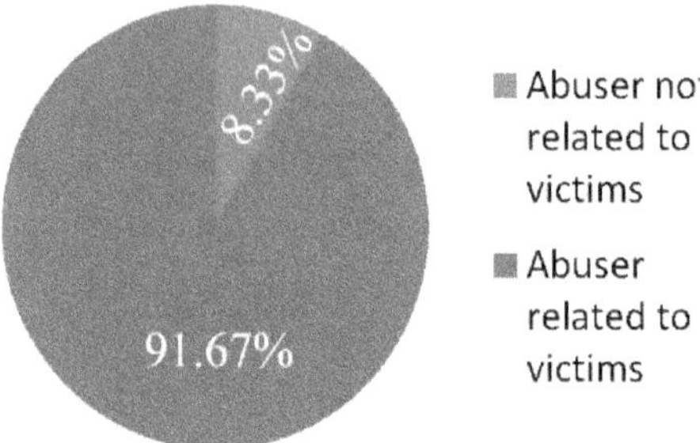

Figure 8
Percentage of abusers who were related to victims

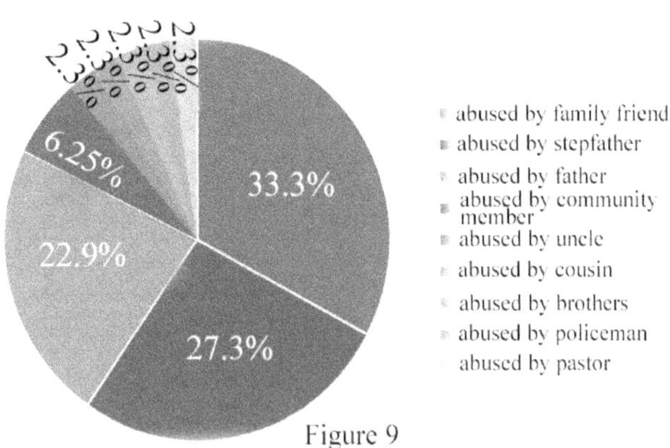

Figure 9
Relationship between abuser and victim. The statistics shows that a total of 77.8% of the abuse happened in the family.

In most cases, the community was not aware of the abuse. However, behavior changes in the victims were evident. There was also an overlapping of these behavioral patterns in some individuals. Respondents cited the following behavior pattern among the abused:

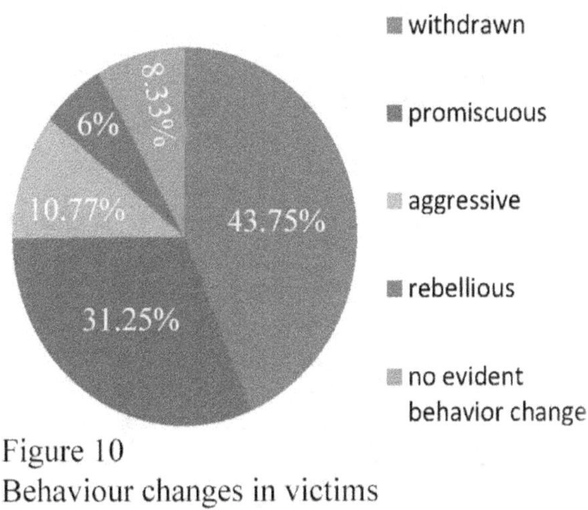

Figure 10
Behaviour changes in victims

Figure 11 shows respondents' belief in the level of church awareness to sexual abuse.

Figure 12 shows how respondents feel about the church addressing the issue of sexual abuse.

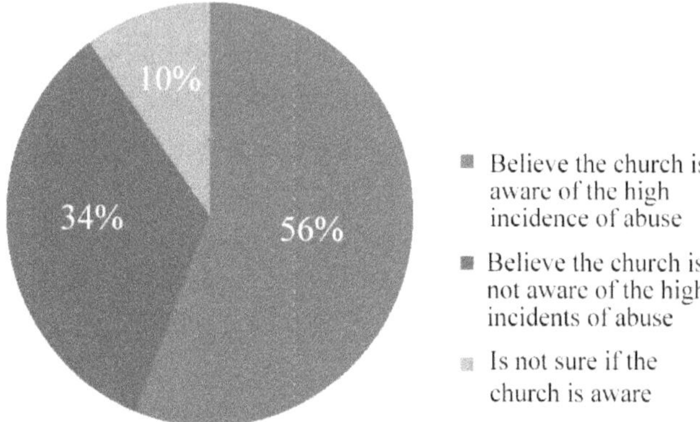

Figure 11. Belief of respondents to church awareness.

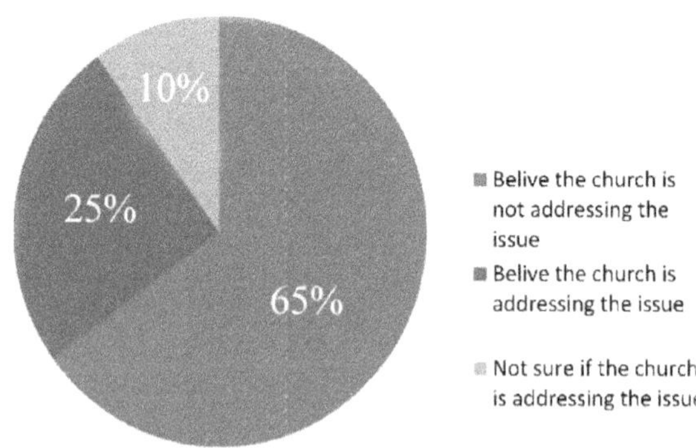

Figure 12. Feelings about the extent to which church is addressing the issue.

Respondents recommended that the church:

(a) Create an atmosphere where people feel like they can trust individuals.
(b) Teach signs of sexual abuse.
(c) Hold forums to address issues of sexual abuse.

Interview Results

Interview (1)[17]

Interviews with members of the police department supplied the following statistics coming out of the Constabulary Resource Centre.

Table 1 shows the number and categories of sexual offenses reported over the period 2000-2008. The number of cases for 2007, however, was not accessible.

Table 2 shows the number of convictions for sexual offenses over the period 2004-2008.

Table 1. Categories/numbers of sexual offenses reported 2004-2008

Year	Rape	Incest	Carnal Abuse	Total
2004	860	42	409	1311
2005	746	14	346	1106
2006	NK	NK	NK	1185
2007	NK	NK	NK	NK
To September 2008	655	34	541	1230
Total Reported Cases minus 2007				4832

[17] Interview with officer at the Constabulary Resource Center, November 1, 2008

Table 2. Convictions (by category) of sexual offenses reported 2000 - 2008

Year	Rape	Incest	Carnal Abuse	Total
2004	62	2	37	101
2005	26	1	27	54
2006	37	5	37	79
2007	26	2	39	67
To June 2008	14	2	24	40
Total Cases Convicted in 2007				341

Figure 13 reports statistics from the Constabulary Resource Centre and provides a visual comparison of sexual abuse cases reported and the number of cases convicted. It should be noted that the conviction rate is only 8.91%.

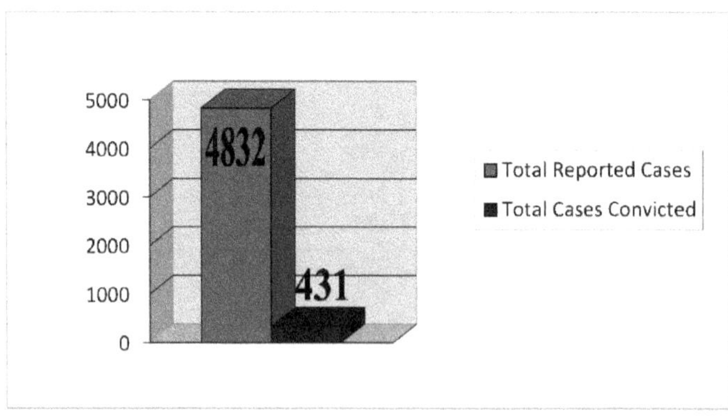

Figure 13. Conviction rate of sexual abuse cases

As is evident from the tables where convictions are concerned, there was an overwhelming decrease in the figures. The officers believe that this is a direct result of victims refusing to come forward to give evidence for varying reasons. One such reason is the fact that victims fear for their lives. Another reason is that victims are coerced into protecting victims, many of whom are family members or some prominent figure in their lives. Another reason is that victims fear ridicule and prefer to keep the abuse a secret.

The officers also explained that the court experience could be very traumatic and embarrassing for some individuals. Hence, some victims forego reporting abuse to avoid the trauma of the trial. These reasons given by the law officers are the very same ones that have perpetuated the culture of silence where sexual abuse is concerned.

Interview (2)[18]

Following the questionnaire session, an unplanned interview was conducted. One of the respondents volunteered to share her testimony for the purpose of this paper. She is thirty years of age and was raped by three men when she was fourteen and still a virgin. She recalled being told by the third man who entered her

[18] Interview with respondent to questionnaire who wanted to share her story for this paper, November 17, 2008

how big her vagina was. The man used very derogatory terms. In spite of the physical pain she felt, the woman reported the man's words to be much more painful; she felt dirty.

She recalled not sharing her experience with anyone for fear that she would be ridiculed. She also felt guilty because she had left her house without her parent's consent. She thought about committing suicide many times but found that she was too much of a coward to carry out her plans. She kept hearing the words of the men echoing in her head and sought comfort from other men. She became very promiscuous. By age twenty, she had lost count of the number of sexual partners she had. She also had two abortions by the time she was twenty.

At age twenty-five, she was introduced to the Lord and became a Christian. However, in church she felt like damaged goods. Her greatest ordeal was hearing ministers preach about fornication or sexual purity. Although she yearned for marriage and family, she resigned herself to the fact that she would never get married because she would not want any of the good church men to get such tarnished property. She would constantly re-live the experience she endured at fourteen years of age, especially at night, and usually cried herself to sleep. Her encounter with the Lord rid her of the desire to return to her old lifestyle. Each day she would wake up, put on her mask, and resign herself to going about her daily chores or church routine.

Her most traumatic experience in the church, however, occurred when a brother from the church (one of the leaders) began to show interest in her. He gave her indications that he was interested in marriage, but she told him outright that she was not good enough for him. He continued to pursue her, and their friendship developed to the point where she could share her experience with him. She expected the relationship to end at that point. However, the church brother only expressed his sympathy and suggested that she see a counselor. Her healing began as she felt free to share her experience with her counselor.

The church brother later joined her in the counseling sessions and was a source of support for her. Today, they are married with two children and share a wonderful life together. This individual has now comforted herself with the thought that God allowed her experience to prepare her for ministry. At present, she works with victims of sexual abuse.

Interview (3)

The story of this woman brings into focus many of the points revealed in interviews with professionals who work with sexually abused victims. Doctor Barrington

Davidson disclosed that victims of child sexual abuse usually carry these scars into adulthood. It is also true that sexual relations in marriage are often affected by child sexual abuse where victims re-live their trauma during sexual relations with their husbands. Doctor Davidson also disclosed that situations exist where a woman freezes or even becomes violent whenever her husband makes sexual advances toward her. This, he says, is not intentional on the part of the women who, in most cases, really feel that they have overcome their trauma. In cases like these, the feelings were only repressed.[19]

Repression is a defense mechanism that blocks or forbids dangerous desires and thoughts from entering one's consciousness. Defense mechanisms protect individuals from anxiety; "they operate unconsciously and distort reality."[20] Doctor Davidson's argument is supported by Clifford and Joyce Penner, who stated that child molestation is the most commonly discussed

---

[19] Interview with Dr. Barrington Davidson, counseling psychologist specializing in marriage and family therapy at Family Life Ministries, a counseling center in Kingston, Jamaica. August 12,2008.

[20] David Sue, Derald Sue, and Stanley Sue, *Understanding Abnormal Behavior* (New York: Haughton Mifflin Company, 1997), 42.

past violation of mutual respect that leaves a scar on the adult's sexual wholeness and can affect sex life.[21]

When asked about the possibility of these individuals being helped, Dr. Davidson answered in the affirmative. However, he stressed the need for professional help. This can be a very long process that may not necessarily yield the desired result, as some individuals have developed chronic psychological disorders as a result of their trauma. Some victims of sexual abuse even have to be confined to psychiatric wards as a result of their trauma and are never again able to live complete lives. Where individuals seem to have developed the ability to cope and want to move on to marriage, professional pre-marital counseling is strongly recommended. Disclosure to the marriage partner is also recommended as this will allow the partner to become sensitive to and work along with the spouse in overcoming any lingering fears.

---

[21] Clifford L. Penner and Joyce J. Penner, *Restoring the Pleasure: Complete Step–by-Step Programs to Help Couples Overcome the most Common Sexual Barriers* (Nashville: W Publishing Group, 1993), 23,117.

Interview (4)[22]

Each of the counselors from the four who were interviewed had between five and ten years of experience working with sexually abused victims. They all expressed the view that although individuals have been abused at different ages in their early childhood years, sexual abuse is most prevalent between the ages of eight and sixteen years. Individuals, however, carry the scars of this abuse into adulthood. In fact, it is usually during adulthood that individuals who are still feeling the pain of their trauma seek counseling in an effort to overcome their pain. Many of these persons carried some form of resentment, not just towards the perpetrator but also towards their parents or caregivers who they felt never allowed for the punishment of their abusers.

Although there were a few isolated cases in which the perpetrators were unknown, in most cases, the abusers were closely associated with the victims. Perpetrators were fathers, stepfathers, siblings, other family members, or friends of the family. Some perpetrators were also influential individuals (pastors, church leaders, teachers, policemen) in the lives of the victims. The counselors were particularly concerned by the number of perpetrators who were pastors or church

[22] Interview with three psychologists, November 13,2008.

leaders. This was cause for concern since this number seems to be on the rise, and these individuals were supposed to uphold moral values. However, family members, many of whom are Christians, seem to be the leading perpetrators in this category.

Another concern expressed by the counselors is that, although some of these sexual malpractices are very current, it is evident that this issue has been in society for several years. This is indicated by the fact that many adults, who come for this sort of counseling, come as a result of the trauma they suffered during their childhood years, which is still having a negative effect on them.

There is evidence to suggest that the population seeking counseling is predominantly people with church affiliations. Intake forms (registration form) filled out by these individuals asks for such information. The counselors find that it is very rare to find one person who is not affiliated with a church. However, counselors feel that the church, to a great extent, is not meeting the needs of these abused individuals. Not only is the church ill-equipped with the resources to deal professionally with the matter of sexual abuse, but sex remains a taboo subject in many church circles. Where any sort of help is offered, it is usually in the spiritual domain, where individuals are encouraged to fast, pray, and read their Bibles in order to overcome their trauma.

The need for psychological intervention is usually not understood or encouraged.

The psychologists agree that the effects of this trauma on the victims vary depending on the individual. One of the most common effects of this trauma is low self-esteem, where individuals lose their self-worth. In some cases, some of these women also abstain from sexual intercourse for the rest of their lives. Among the reasons for this decision is the fear of men, a feeling of inadequacy, or the fear of being tarnished in some way.

These women also suffer from guilt and shame as they often find some reason to blame their own selves for the abuse they suffered. An attitude of mistrust also develops, particularly as it relates to members of the opposite sex. This can also lead to the development of paranoid personality disorder. This causes individuals to become overly suspicious. This is not necessarily a suspicion of members of the opposite sex. Instead, individuals become suspicious of anyone they see talking because they feel that they are the ones being discussed.

Individuals can become so depressed that they develop suicidal thoughts. Individuals are also known to become promiscuous as they seek to affirm their value to the opposite sex. Promiscuity also allows for their sexual needs to be met without their emotions getting involved. Victims are also known to display severe anger problems and mood swings. Frigidity can also develop as a direct result of this trauma. Women are usually unaware of this condition until they marry or get involved in a sexual relationship and panic sets in.

One of the psychologists describes an effect as a condition in which victims re-live the actual abuse. Clients are known to actually replay the scene, displaying the very behavior that they displayed at the time of the abuse. The counselor or anyone in the presence at this time of the "replay" is perceived as the abuser.

The most surprising information shared, however, is the relationship between sexual abuse and homosexuality. Some women are known to become lesbians as a result of being sexually abused by men. They seek sexual gratification and comfort from members of the same sex as they find men repulsive. The statistics in Figure 14 show the findings where the relationship between lesbianism and sexual abuse is concerned. Of six lesbian clients seen by one counselor, five were sexually abused by a male in their childhood years. Of four lesbian clients seen by another counselor, all were sexually abused as a child. Ninety percent of the clients who were lesbians were therefore sexually abused by men.

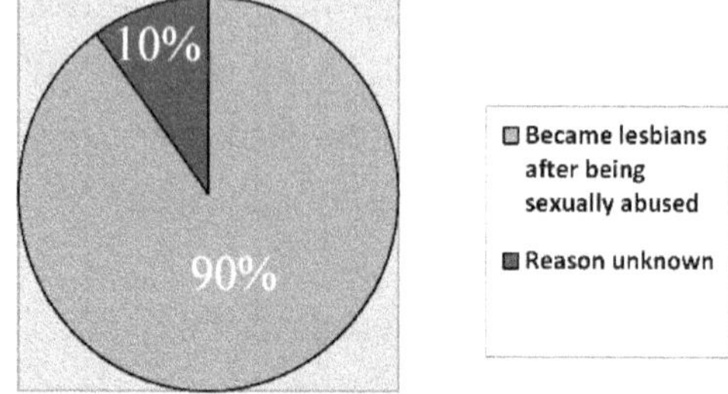

Figure 14.
Percentage of women who became lesbians after being sexually abused.

Research Conclusion

The interaction with other writers by way of the research conducted, the questionnaires completed, as well as the interviews conducted, have much in common. The effects of sexual abuse on individuals are many and can have severe implications. Sexual abuse is most common within the age group classified as children (70%). It is also evident that this abuse is most prevalent within the family setting or is perpetrated by individuals who have gained family trust, thus allowing for most cases to go unreported.

A total of 92.7% of sexual abuse is committed by individuals who are close to victims. In fact, given the vast number of cases that are never reported, the figures provided by the Jamaican police department indicate that the number of victims related to or knowing their abusers is far greater in reality. The 8.91% conviction given by the police department, therefore, is far less in reality. There is definitely a culture of silence surrounding sexual abuse. The silence has encouraged the age-old practice from generation to generation. Therefore, the true magnitude of this problem has not been ascertained. The church, for the most part, is not able to adequately meet the needs of the survivors of sexual abuse.

In examining sexual abuse from a scriptural perspective, it is discovered that God was not silent on the issue. God intervened in person, as in the case of Hagar, or through other individuals, as in the case of Bathsheba and Nathan. God is working through the church today. In fact, the church is called to be God's ambassadors (see 2 Corinthians 5:20). The church therefore needs to have programs in place for the sexual abuse victims in order to serve this population that represents a wide cross-section of our ministry setting.

As was previously mentioned, the positions of Karl Bath and David Bosh apply here; the theology of the church in our society needs to be relevant to our setting. Our Bible studies, for instance, should encourage people to be sensitive to the trauma suffered by these sexually abused women of old and develop empathy for the women in our present culture. This should lead to planning church programs that will address their needs. At the same time, this will allow God's defense of these persons to be evident, and we will fulfill our mandate to be God's image bearers. In this way, the church becomes aware of its responsibilities to those who have endured sexual abuse, and plan strategies for dealing with the problem. This is specifically applicable to church institutions where their Sunday School Manual and other study literature, for instance, are prepared in an American setting. Although Jamaica shares much in common with other cultures, we need to make our study literature more culturally specific so the needs of those in our society are addressed.

Public Presentation and Response

In discussing the findings of the research with my group, most persons were not surprised about the existence of hurting women due to sexual abuse. However, the percentage of those who felt that the church must put measures in place to ensure that the culture of silence is broken was alarmingly low.

In examining the large percentage of women who were abused within the confines of the home, it is evident that there needs to be a strong family life program that teaches family members their roles and responsibilities and holds them accountable. The whole matter of sexual abuse and its effects should be integrated into a family life program, using victims who are Bible characters as examples for learning about the impact of sexual abuse. The need for honest communication between children and their caregivers should be stressed. Further, the church should not assume that people know how to engage in open and effective communication.

Communication skills should be taught, and caregivers should be able to read the non-verbal cues of those for whom they care. Sex education should also be a major part of a family life program. Individuals need to learn about their sexuality. Given the age at which children become victims of sexual abuse, it is critical for children to learn about their sexuality at an early age and be sensitized to what is inappropriate sexual behavior. Children should be made aware of all avenues available to them for support and be encouraged to always turn to the resources for help. Caregivers should also be educated about the signs and symptoms of sexual abuse.

Although the church should have a strong family life program, it should not be left solely to the family to ensure that their children are protected from sexual predators. The church has also been given a cultural mandate. Given the strong culture of silence that exists, particularly as it relates to sexual abuse within the family, there should be an effective children's ministry program in each church that advocates for the least of the least. Children's ministry leaders should be trained in understanding young minds and should be very sensitive to changes in the behavior of these children that signal emotional problems related to sexual abuse.

When behavioral changes are observed, individuals should be referred for professional help, whether abuse is suspected or identified. The church that does not have professional counselors should, therefore, be aware of the different agencies or institutions that offer professional services for victims of sexual abuse. Where referrals are needed, individuals should be trained as to how to make proper referrals.

Because pastors are among the perpetrators of sexual abuse, persons who enroll in ministry should be required to undergo a psychological assessment and a period of counseling prior to entering ministry. Ministers should also be assessed periodically, giving every individual who relates to the minister a chance to take part in the assessment process. This will not only equip pastors with self-assessment skills and allow them to better understand their own sexuality, but it will also allow them to become sensitive to other areas of weakness and make conscious efforts to address them. Pastors will also be sensitized to the need to be engaged in ongoing training and therapy for church workers.

Workers should be familiar with the rape crisis intervention services in communities so that they make appropriate referrals when necessary. Most programs should advocate and not only facilitate the delivery of these services. Help to protect the survivor from secondary victimization by promoting positive interactions with other professionals. Rape crisis centers also provide survivors with information about available services and resources, promote social support, provide psycho-education regarding common reactions to sexual assault, and offer options to facilitate a survivor's ability to make informed decisions during this difficult time in his or her life (Levers, 2012).

Conclusion

The evidence suggests that the church, for whatever reason, does not place adequate emphasis on stemming sexual abuse in Jamaican society and changing the attitudes towards sexual abuse. Although it is not possible to make an anumerical comparison between the occurrences of sexual abuse among God's chosen people and God's people today, the emotional traumas and upheavals are very much the same today as they were in Egypt, Canaan, and Palestine. The situation today is still giving rise to emotional instability in women, some who, like Hagar, have to parent their children alone or, like Tamar, who in spite of pleading with the family, have to bear their shame and be resigned to a life of the recluse. There are some women who, like Bathsheba, just have to work with the plan. The culture of silence continues to prevail, and women continue to suffer their emotional turmoil, often alone.

All the findings support the claim that sexual abuse has far-reaching implications and that many victims of sexual abuse continue to suffer in spite of the fact that they are in the church, which should be a place of healing. It has been proven that the whole matter of sexual abuse is not a denominational problem but a body of Christ problem. The onus is therefore on the church to have an ecumenical approach to ministry and put programs in place to deal with sexual abuse, not just at a denominational level but also at a societal level. This will ensure that the needs of the entire community are met.

The church also has a responsibility to make its ministry relevant to its setting. With the high incidence of this occurrence in our society, tackling sexual abuse is very relevant to the Jamaican societal problem.

Could it be that given the findings of this research, the needs of the greater cross-section of the Caribbean church is not being met, particularly bearing in mind that women make up the vast majority of the Jamaican church? There is much more work for the church to do in making our ministry relevant to our setting.

Appendix 1

Questionnaire

Age:
16-20 years [ ] 20-25 years [ ] 25-30 years [ ]
Over 30 years [ ]

Gender:
Male [ ] Female [ ]

Position in Church:
Leader [ ] Member [ ] Visitor [ ]

Do you know of any girl/woman who has ever been sexually abused?
Yes [ ] No [ ]

If yes, how old was she?
0-7 years [ ] 8-16 years [ ] 17-25 [ ] 25-30 years [ ]
over 30 years [ ]

Was this reported to anyone?
Yes [ ] No [ ] Do not know [ ]

If yes, who was this reported to?

____

____

How was this dealt with?

____

____

Do you know who the perpetrator was?
Yes [ ] No [ ]

Was the perpetrator related to victim in any way?
Yes [ ] No [ ]

If yes, in what way?
Family member [ ] Family friend [ ]
Church leader [ ] Stranger [ ] Other [ ]

Please specify

____

____

How was the perpetrator dealt with?
Nothing was done [ ] Arrested [ ] Counselled [ ]
Other [ ]

Please specify

____

____

____

____

Were individuals in the community aware of this situation?
Yes [ ] No [ ]

If yes, what was their reaction towards:

The victim:

____

____

____

____

The perpetrator:

____

____

____

____

Did you notice any change in the behavior of the individual who was abused?
Yes [ ] No [ ]

If yes, what change did you notice?

Individual became withdrawn [ ]
Individual became promiscuous [ ]
Individual became aggressive [ ]
Individual became rebellious [ ]
Other[ ]

Please specify:

____

____

____

____

Do you believe the church is showing enough awareness of the high incidence of sexual abuse in society?
Yes [ ] No [ ]

Do you see the church making an effort to address this situation?
Yes [ ] No [ ]

If yes, in what way?

____

____

____

____

What recommendation would you make to the church where sexual abuse is concerned?

____

____

____

____

____

____

____

____

Appendix 2

Interview Questions

How long have you been working with victims of sexual abuse?

____

____

In what age group is sexual abuse most prevalent?

____

____

Are the perpetrators usually known to the victims?

____

____

In what categories do perpetrators fall, and which category is most frequent?

____

____

What are the effects (long term/short term) of this trauma on victims?

____

____

Do you find this situation to be prevalent among church people?

____

____

How do you see the church dealing with this situation?

____

____

What recommendation would you make to the church in addressing this situation?

____

____

____

____

____

____

Bibliography

Ammicht-Quinn, Regina, Hille Hacker and Maureen Lunker-Kenney, eds. *The Structural Betrayal of Trust.* London: SCM Press, 2004.

Bailey, K. E. *Women in Ben Sera and the New Testament.* Cleveland: Dillon/Lieder Bach, 1972.

Barth Karl. *Church Dogmatics: The Doctrine of Reconciliation*, 1 V.3.2. Eds. G.W.Bromiley and T.F. Torrance. New York: T&T Clark International, 2004.

Beckford, George L. *Persistent Poverty: Underdevelopment in Plantation Economics.* New York: Oxford University Press, 1972.

Bosch, David J. *Transforming Mission-Paradigm Shifts in Theology of Mission.* New York: Orbis Books, 1999.

Cooper-White, Pamela. *The Cry of Tamar: Violence Against Women and the Church's Response.* Minneapolis: Fortress Press, 1995.

Davis, Patricia. *Counseling Adolescent Girls.* Minneapolis: Augsburg Fortress, 1996.

Frieberg, Niels C. and Mark R. Laaser. *Before the Fall, Preventing Pastoral Sexual Abuse*. Minnesota: Liturgical Press,1998.

Grenz, Stanley J. and Roy D. Bell. *Betrayal of Trust: Sexual Misconduct in the Pastorate.* Downers Grove: Intervarsity Press, 1995.

Hedges, Gott, *Sexual Abuse: Pastoral Responses.* ed. Daniel G. Bagsby. Nashville: Intervarsity Press, 2004

Kerney, Timothy. *Caring for Sexually Abused Children: A Handbook for Families and Churches.* Downers Grove: Intervarsity Press, 1995.

Letman, Michelle-Ann. 2008. Carnal Abuse Hush Up: Fear Culture of Silence Hinders Persecution, *Daily Gleaner*, August 19.

Levers, L. L. (2012). *Trauma counseling: Theories and interventions*. New York:

MacFarlane, Kee. *Sexual Abuse of Young Children*. London: The Guilford Press, 1986.

Metzger, Bruce M. and Roland E. Murphy, eds. *New Revised Standard Version, the New Annotated Bible with Apocrypha*. New York: Oxford University Press, 1994.

Miller, Alice. *Breaking Down the Wall of Silence: The Liberating Experience of Facing Painful Truth.* New York: Meridian, 1997.

O'Grady, Ron. *The Hidden Shame of the Church; Sexual Abuse of Children and the Church.* Switzerland: WCC Publication, 2001.

Ormerod, Neil and Thea Ormerod. *When Ministers Sin: Sexual Abuse in the Church.* Alexandria: Millennium Books, 1995.

Penner, Joyce J. and Clifford L Penner. *Counseling for Sexual Disorder*. Nashville: Thomas Nelson, 2005.

Penner, Clifford and Joyce Penner. *Restoring the Pleasure-Complete Step by Step Programs to Help couples overcome the most common Sexual Barriers*. Nashville: Thomas Nelson, 1993.

Poling, Nancy Werking, ed. *Victim to Survivor: Women Recovering from Clergy Sexual Abuse.* Cleveland: United Church Press, 1999.

Ragsdale, Katherine Hancock. *Boundary Walls-Intimacy and Distance in Healing Relationships.* Cleveland: The Pilgrim Press, 1996.

Read, Wendy. *A Conspiracy of Love: Living Through and Beyond Childhood Sexual Abuse.* Kelowna, BC: Northstone,1953.

Rediger, G. Lloyd. *Beyond the Scandals: A Guide to Healthy Sexuality for Clergy.* Minneapolis: Fortress Press, 2003.

Smith. Raymond T. "Social Stratification, Cultural Pluralism and Integration in West Indian Societies," in S. Lewis and T.G. Matthews (eds.), Caribbean Integration (Rio Piedras: Puerto Rico,1967)

Spangler, Annand Jean E. Syswerda. *Women of the Bible.* Grand Rapids: Zondervan, 2007.

Sue, David, Derald Sue and Stanley Sue. *Understanding Abnormal Behavior.* USA: Haughton Mifflin Company, 1997.

Whitehead, James D. and Evelyn Eaton Whitehead. *Method in Ministry, Theological Reflections and Christian Ministry.* San Francisco: Harper & Row Publishers, 1980.

Williams, Deloris. *Sisters in the Wilderness.* New York: Orbis Books. 1993

Winnebrenner, Jan and Debra Frazier. *When A Leader Fails. What Happens to Everyone Else?* Minneapolis: Bethany House Publishers, 1993.

www.ingramcontent.com/pod-product-compliance
Lightning Source LLC
LaVergne TN
LVHW010119170826
845678LV00012B/2495